LIMERICKS

AN OFF-COLOUR ADULT COLOURING BOOK

THERE was a young LADY of HARROW

ISBN-13: 978-1540665522
ISBN-10: 1540665526

THERE WAS A YOUNG LADY OF HARROW.
WHO COMPLAINED THAT HER CUNT WAS TOO NARROW,
FOR TIMES WITHOUT NUMBER
SHE WOULD USE A CUCUMBER,
BUT COULD NOT ACCOMPLISH A MARROW.

Illustrate Your Limerick:

Finish This Limerick:

Line 1: __THERE ONCE WAS A MAN FROM PERU__

Line 2: _____

Line 3: _____

Line 4: _____

Line 5: _____

THERE WAS A YOUNG LADY OF GLASGOW,
AND FONDLY HER LOVER DID ASK, "OH,
PRAY ALLOW ME A FUCK,"
BUT SHE SAID, "NO, MY DUCK,
BUT YOU MAY, IF YOU PLEASE, UP MY ARSE GO."

Illustrate Your Limerick:

Finish This Limerick:

Line 1: **THERE WAS AN ODD FELLOW NAMED GUS**

Line 2: _____

Line 3: _____

Line 4: _____

Line 5: _____

THERE WAS A YOUNG MAN HAD THE ART
OF MAKING A CAPITAL TART,
WITH A HANDFUL OF SHIT,
SOME SNOT AND A SPIT,
AND HE'D FLAVOR THE WHOLE WITH A FART.

Illustrate Your Limerick:

Finish This Limerick:

Line 1: **THERE ONCE WAS A MAN FROM TIBET** _____

Line 2: _____

Line 3: _____

Line 4: _____

Line 5: _____

THERE WAS AN OLD MAN OF CONNAUGHT.
WHOSE PRICK WAS REMARKABLY SHORT,
WHEN HE GOT INTO BED
THE OLD WOMAN SAID,
"THIS ISN'T A PRICK, IT'S A WART."

Illustrate Your Limerick:

Finish This Limerick:

Line 1: __THERE ONCE WAS A MAN STUCK IN A STALL__

Line 2: _____

Line 3: _____

Line 4: _____

Line 5: _____

THERE WAS A GAY COUNTESS OF BRAY,
AND YOU MAY THINK IT ODD WHEN I SAY,
THAT IN SPITE OF HIGH STATION,
RANK AND EDUCATION,
SHE ALWAYS SPELT CUNT WITH A K.

Illustrate Your Limerick:

Finish This Limerick:

Line 1: **THERE WAS AN ENCHANTING YOUNG BRIDE**

Line 2: _____

Line 3: _____

Line 4: _____

Line 5: _____

THERE WAS AN OLD PARSON OF LUNDY,
FELL ASLEEP IN HIS VESTRY ON SUNDAY;
HE AWOKE WITH A SCREAM,
"WHAT, ANOTHER WET DREAM,
THIS COMES OF NOT FRIGGING SINCE MONDAY."

Illustrate Your Limerick:

Finish This Limerick:

Line 1: __I ONCE FELL IN LOVE WITH A blONDE__

Line 2: _____

Line 3: _____

Line 4: _____

Line 5: _____

THERE WAS A STRONG MAN OF DRUMRIG,
WHO ONE DAY DID SEVEN TIMES FRIG:
HE BUGGERED THREE SAILORS,
FOUR JEWS AND TWO TAILORS,
AND ENDED BY FUCKING A PIG.

Illustrate Your Limerick:

Finish This Limerick:

Line 1: __THERE ONCE WAS A GIRL CALLED JANE__

Line 2: _____

Line 3: _____

Line 4: _____

Line 5: _____

THERE WAS AN OLD MAN OF THE MOUNTAIN.
WHO FRIGGED HIMSELF INTO A FOUNTAIN,
FIFTEEN TIMES HAD HE SPENT,
STILL HE WASN'T CONTENT.
HE SIMPLY GOT TIRED OF THE COUNTING.

Illustrate Your Limerick:

Finish This Limerick:

Line 1: **I ONCE HAD A GERBIL NAMED BOBBY**

Line 2: _____

Line 3: _____

Line 4: _____

Line 5: _____

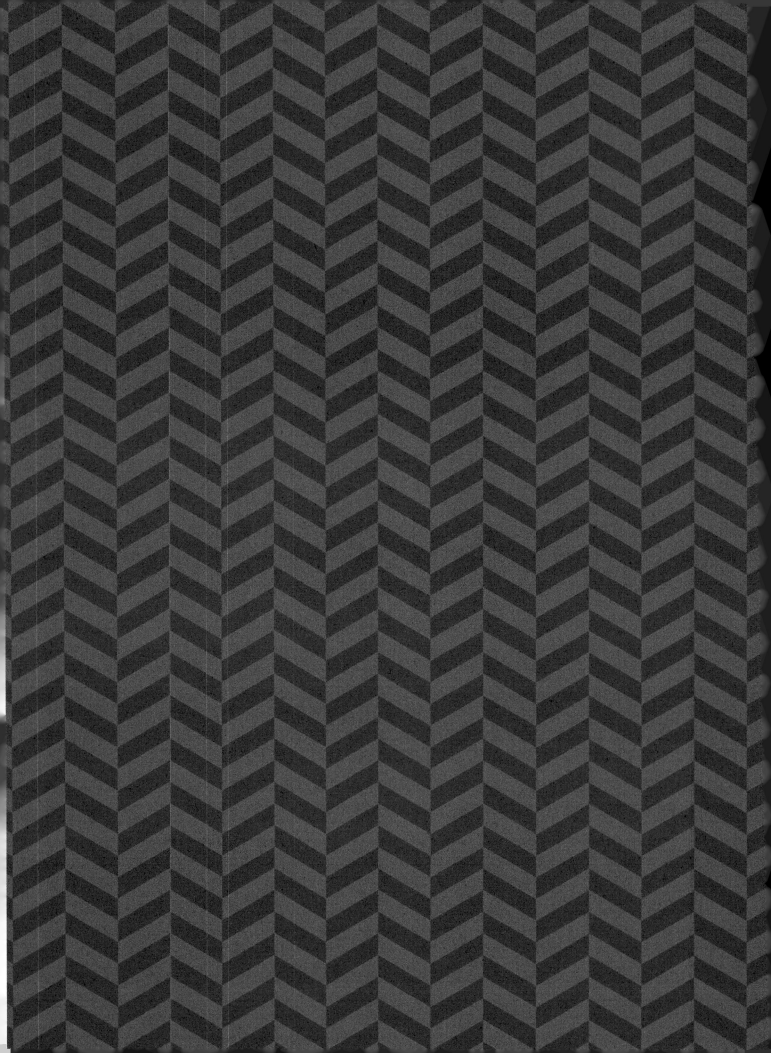

THERE WAS A YOUNG MAN OF NANTUCKET,
WHO WENT DOWN A WELL IN A BUCKET;
THE LAST WORDS HE SPOKE,
BEFORE THE ROPE BROKE,
WERE, "ARSEHOLE, YOU BUGGER, AND SUCK IT."

Illustrate Your Limerick:

Finish This Limerick:

Line 1: **AN AMBITIOUS YOUNG FELLOW NAMED MATT**

Line 2: _____

Line 3: _____

Line 4: _____

Line 5: _____

A NATIVE OF HAVRE DE GRACE
ONCE TIRED OF CUNT, SAID "I'LL TRY ARSE."
HE UNFOLDED HIS PLAN
TO ANOTHER YOUNG MAN,
WHO SAID, "MOST DECIDEDLY, MY ARSE!"

Illustrate Your Limerick:

Finish This Limerick:

Line 1: **THERE WAS A YOUNG PERSON CALLED SMARTY**

Line 2: _____

Line 3: _____

Line 4: _____

Line 5: _____

THERE WAS A YOUNG MAN OF CALCUTTA
WHO THOUGHT HE WOULD DO A SMART TRICK:
SO ANOINTED HIS ARSEHOLE WITH BUTTER.
AND IN IT INSERTED HIS PRICK.

Illustrate Your Limerick:

Finish This Limerick:

Line 1: AN ELDERLY MAN CALLED KEITH

Line 2: _____

Line 3: _____

Line 4: _____

Line 5: _____

IT WAS NOT FOR GREED AFTER GOLD;
IT WAS NOT FOR THIRST AFTER PELF;
'TWAS SIMPLY BECAUSE HE'D BEEN TOLD
TO BLOODY WELL BUGGER HIMSELF.

Illustrate Your Limerick:

Finish This Limerick:

Line 1: THERE ONCE WAS A GIRL FROM DUBAI

Line 2: _____

Line 3: _____

Line 4: _____

Line 5: _____

THERE WAS A YOUNG LASS OF DALKEITH,
WHO FRIGGED A YOUNG MAN WITH HER TEETH;
SHE COMPLAINED THAT HE STUNK;
NOT SO MUCH FROM THE SPUNK;
BUT HIS ARSEHOLE WAS JUST UNDERNEATH.

Illustrate Your Limerick:

Finish This Limerick:

Line 1: **THERE WAS A YOUNG FELLOW NAMED CLYDE**

Line 2: _____

Line 3: _____

Line 4: _____

Line 5: _____

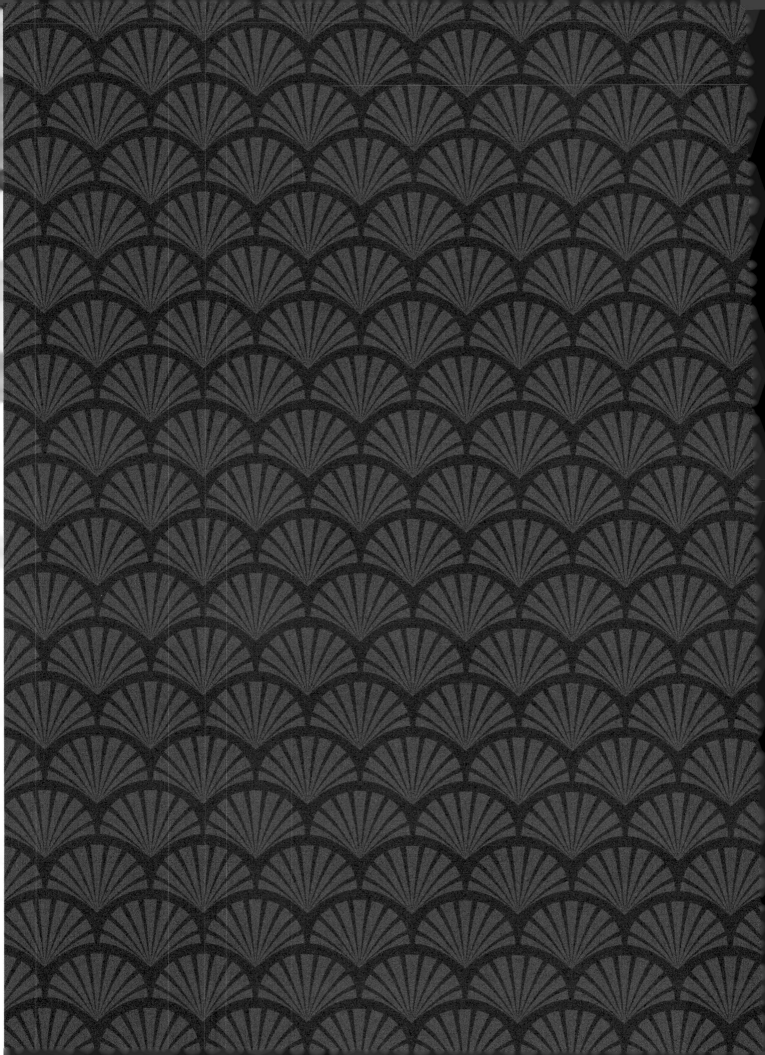

THERE WAS A GAY PARSON OF NORTON,
WHOSE PRICK, ALTHOUGH THICK, WAS A SHORT 'UN;
TO MAKE UP FOR THIS LOSS,
HE HAD BALLS LIKE A HORSE,
AND NEVER SPENT LESS THAN A QUARTERN.

Illustrate Your Limerick:

Finish This Limerick:

Line 1: __AN INTREPID EXPLORER NAMED PETTY__

Line 2: _____

Line 3: _____

Line 4: _____

Line 5: _____

THERE WAS A YOUNG MAN OF THE TWEED.
WHO SUCKED HIS WIFE'S ARSE THRO' A REED;
WHEN SHE HAD DIARRHEA.
HE'D LET NONE COME NEAR.
FOR FEAR THEY SHOULD POACH ON HIS FEED.

Illustrate Your Limerick:

Finish This Limerick:

Line 1: THERE WAS AN OLD MAN IN A BOAT

Line 2:

Line 3:

Line 4:

Line 5:

THERE WAS AN OLD MAN OF BALBRIGGAN,
WHO CUNT JUICE WAS FREQUENTLY SWIGGING;
BUT EVEN TO THIS,
HE PREFERRED TOM-CAT'S PISS,
WHICH HE KEPT A POX'D MELON TO FRIG IN.

Illustrate Your Limerick:

Finish This Limerick:

Line 1: __THERE WAS AN OLD MAN WITH A GONG__

Line 2: _____

Line 3: _____

Line 4: _____

Line 5: _____

A CABMAN WHO DROVE IN BIARRITZ,
ONCE FRIGHTENED A FARE INTO FITS;
WHEN REPROV'D FOR A FART,
HE SAID, "GOD BLESS MY HEART
WHEN I BREAK WIND I USUALLY SHITS."

Illustrate Your Limerick:

Finish This Limerick:

Line 1: I MET HER IN CHAT, SHE WAS NEAT,

Line 2: _____

Line 3: _____

Line 4: _____

Line 5: _____

A YOUNG WOMAN GOT MARRIED AT CHESTER.
HER MOTHER SHE KISSED AND SHE BLESSED HER.
SAYS SHE, "YOU'RE IN LUCK,
HE'S A STUNNING GOOD FUCK.
FOR I'VE HAD HIMSELF MYSELF DOWN IN LEICESTER.

Illustrate Your Limerick:

Finish This Limerick:

Line 1: THERE ONCE WAS A YOUNG MAN CALLED KYLE

Line 2: _____

Line 3: _____

Line 4: _____

Line 5: _____

THERE ONCE WAS A YOUNG MAN OF BULGARIA,
WHO ONCE WENT TO PISS DOWN AN AREA,
SAID MARY TO COOK:
"OH, DO COME AND LOOK,
DID YOU EVER SEE ANYTHING HAIRIER?"

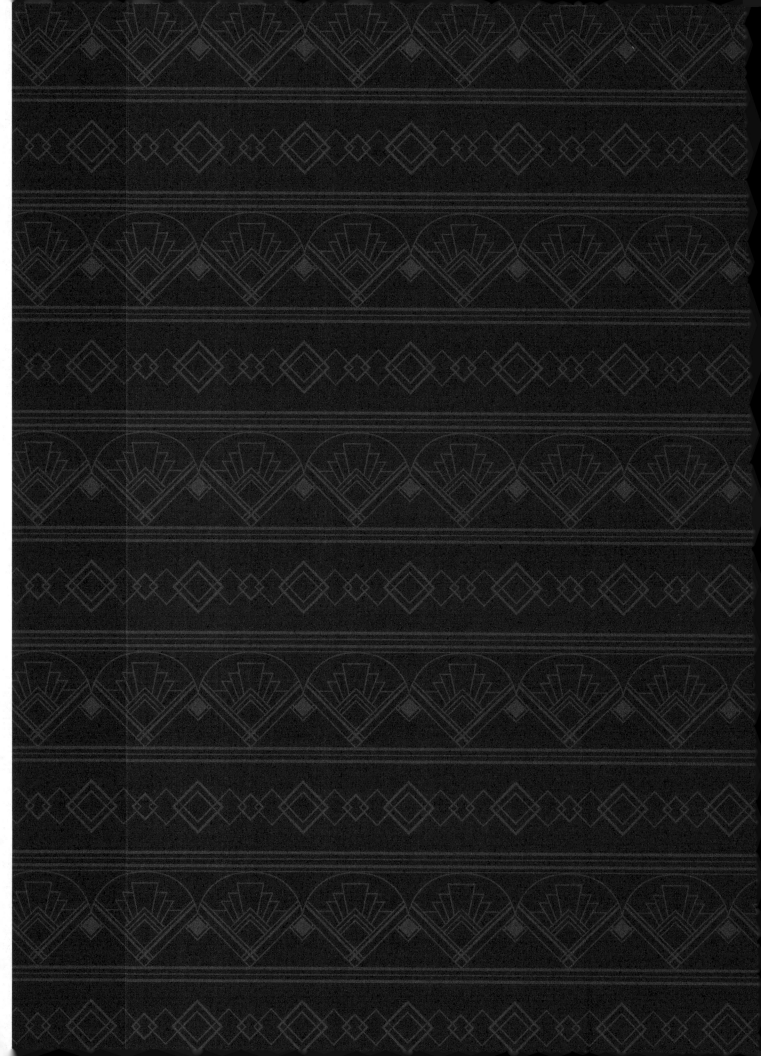

Illustrate Your Limerick:

Finish This Limerick:

Line 1: **I'M PAPERING WALLS IN THE LOO**

Line 2: _____

Line 3: _____

Line 4: _____

Line 5: _____

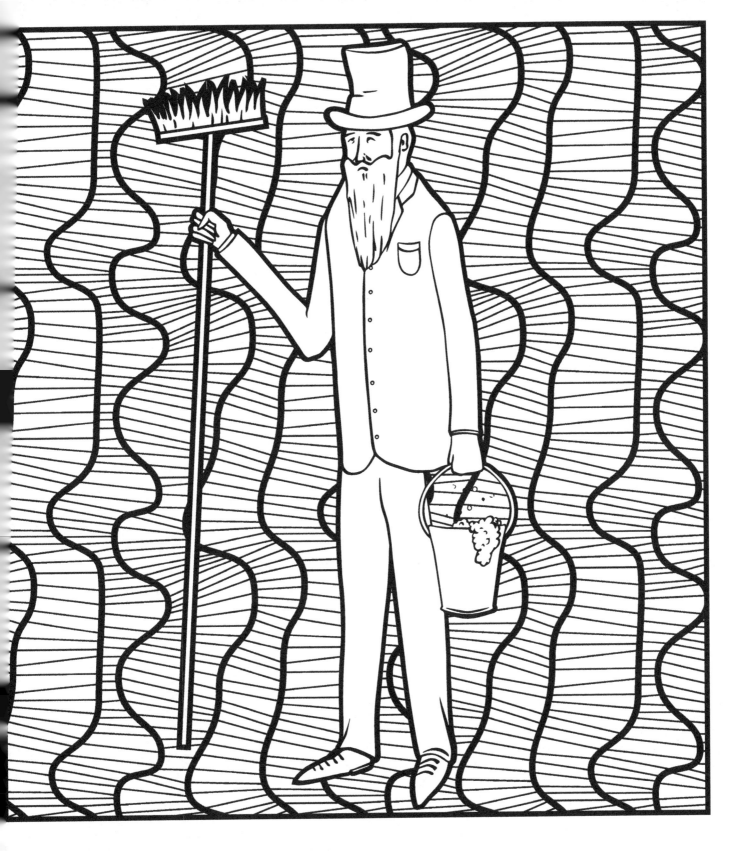

THERE WAS AN OLD MAN FROM GOSHAM,
WHO TOOK OUT HIS BALLS TO WASH 'EM,
HIS WIFE SAID "JACK!
IF YOU DON'T PUT 'EM BACK,
I'LL STAND ON THE FUCKERS AND SQUASH 'EM!"

Illustrate Your Limerick:

Finish This Limerick:

Line 1: **THERE ONCE WAS A BARMAID NAMED GALE**

Line 2:

Line 3:

Line 4:

Line 5:

THERE ONCE WAS A MAN FROM LEEDS,
WHO SWALLOWED A PACKET OF SEEDS,
WITHIN HALF AN HOUR,
HIS DICK WAS A FLOWER,
AND HIS BALLS WERE ALL COVERED WITH WEEDS.

Illustrate Your Limerick:

Finish This Limerick:

Line 1: __THERE ONCE WAS A MAN FROM NANTUCKET__

Line 2: _____

Line 3: _____

Line 4: _____

Line 5: _____

THERE ONCE WAS A LASS FROM KILKENNY,
WHOSE USUAL PRICE WAS A PENNY,
FOR HALF OF THAT SUM,
YOU COULD FINGER HER BUM,
AND HAVE MONEY LEFT OVER FOR DENNY'S.

Illustrate Your Limerick:

Finish This Limerick:

Line 1: _____ THERE WAS A YOUNG GIRL OF CAPE COD _____

Line 2: _____

Line 3: _____

Line 4: _____

Line 5: _____

THERE ONCE WAS A MAN FROM WINSOCKET,
WHO RODE DOWN THE STREET ON A ROCKET,
THE FORCE OF THE BLAST,
BLEW HIS BALLS UP HIS ASS,
AND HIS PECKER WAS FOUND IN HIS POCKET.

Illustrate Your Limerick:

Finish This Limerick:

Line 1: THERE WAS A YOUNG SAILOR NAMED BATES

Line 2:

Line 3:

Line 4:

Line 5:

IN THE GARDEN OF EDEN SAT ADAM,
MASSAGING THE BUST OF HIS MADAM,
HE CHUCKLED WITH MIRTH,
FOR HE KNEW THAT ON EARTH,
THERE WERE ONLY TWO BOOBS AND HE HAD 'EM.

Illustrate Your Limerick:

Finish This Limerick:

Line 1: THERE WAS A YOUNG LADY NAMED WHITE

Line 2:

Line 3:

Line 4:

Line 5:

THERE WAS A YOUNG CHAP FROM OUT YONDER,
WHO BUGGERED A BIG ANACONDA,
HE REGRETTED THIS CRIME,
FOR THE REST OF HIS TIME,
WHILE THE REPTILE GREW FONDER AND FONDER.

Illustrate Your Limerick:

Finish This Limerick:

Line 1: __THERE WAS A YOUNG FELLOW NAMED BLISS__

Line 2: _____

Line 3: _____

Line 4: _____

Line 5: _____

BE SURE TO FOLLOW US
ON SOCIAL MEDIA FOR THE
LATEST GIVEAWAYS & DISCOUNTS

CHECK OUT OUR OTHER BOOKS!

www.honeybadgercoloring.com

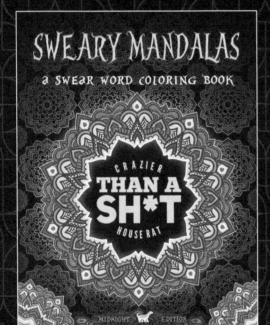

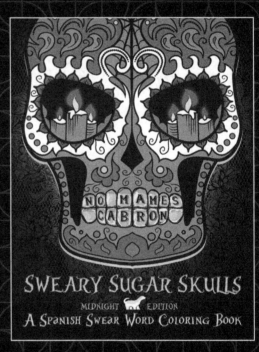

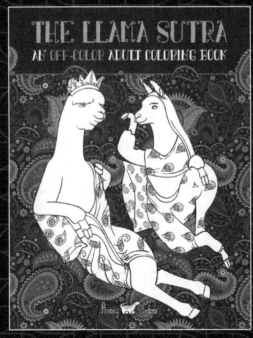

Made in the USA
Las Vegas, NV
21 August 2022